This
Blank Sticker Book

Belongs To:

. . . .

My Lovely Stickers

My Lovely Stickers

My Lovely Stickers

My Lovely Stickers

My Lovely Stickers

My Lovely Stickers

My Lovely Stickers

My Lovely Stickers

My Lovely Stickers

My Lovely Stickers

My Lovely Stickers

My Lovely Stickers

My Lovely Stickers

My Lovely Stickers

My Lovely Stickers

My Lovely Stickers

My Lovely Stickers

My Lovely Stickers

My Lovely Stickers

My Lovely Stickers

My Lovely Stickers

My Lovely Stickers

My Lovely Stickers

My Lovely Stickers

My Lovely Stickers

My Lovely Stickers

My Lovely Stickers

My Lovely Stickers

My Lovely Stickers

My Lovely Stickers

My Lovely Stickers

My Lovely Stickers

My Lovely Stickers

My Lovely Stickers

My Lovely Stickers

My Lovely Stickers

My Lovely Stickers

My Lovely Stickers

My Lovely Stickers

My Lovely Stickers

My Lovely Stickers

My Lovely Stickers

My Lovely Stickers

My Lovely Stickers

My Lovely Stickers

My Lovely Stickers

My Lovely Stickers

My Lovely Stickers

My Lovely Stickers

My Lovely Stickers

My Lovely Stickers

My Lovely Stickers

My Lovely Stickers

My Lovely Stickers

My Lovely Stickers

My Lovely Stickers

My Lovely Stickers

My Lovely Stickers

My Lovely Stickers

My Lovely Stickers

My Lovely Stickers

My Lovely Stickers

My Lovely Stickers

My Lovely Stickers

My Lovely Stickers

My Lovely Stickers

My Lovely Stickers

My Lovely Stickers

My Lovely Stickers

My Lovely Stickers

My Lovely Stickers

My Lovely Stickers

My Lovely Stickers

My Lovely Stickers

My Lovely Stickers

My Lovely Stickers

My Lovely Stickers

My Lovely Stickers

My Lovely Stickers

My Lovely Stickers

My Lovely Stickers

My Lovely Stickers

My Lovely Stickers

My Lovely Stickers

My Lovely Stickers

My Lovely Stickers

My Lovely Stickers

My Lovely Stickers

My Lovely Stickers

My Lovely Stickers

My Lovely Stickers

My Lovely Stickers

My Lovely Stickers

My Lovely Stickers

My Lovely Stickers

My Lovely Stickers

My Lovely Stickers

My Lovely Stickers

My Lovely Stickers